CHAOS AND BUTTERFLIES

Chaos and Butterflies

a poetry collection

ALEXANDRA FREUND

Pearl Press

chaos and butterflies

life contradicts itself with the
perpetual fire of its ebb and flow
and a painted lady fans the flame

the captain goes down

saltwater spills across the deck
waves staining pale wood black
dark depths seeping into cracks
rotting from the inside out
whirlpooling round and round and round
piloting this ship in a bottle
but the glass ceiling can't be cracked

sad (seasonal affective disorder)

pint-sized pearls of rain
coat my bleary windshield in the morning
not quite a cloudburst but
the sky is stone and plain

Los Angeles is mourning the summer she once knew
when mint chip melted on boardwalks
bleeding violet and gold from above
there was no such thing as June gloom

my shoulders miss being freckled and pink
toes craving the cool dip of pool
now the water just reflects my spirit
I'm floating, coasting, pray I don't sink

super blue moon

there was a super blue moon tonight
and I felt my feet tethered to the floor

I'm just a girl on a rock
with contradicting feelings
the moon makes me feel small
like my problems aren't really that big
or is it that I'm insignificant?

I tried to take a picture but the glass was smudged and dirty
though my eyes could see its beauty
and maybe that's enough

if only I looked at the world
as romantically as the universe

renaissance embrace

Donatello sculpted your arms for me
from the slope of a shoulder
to the veins in each wrist
my crown rests in the crook of your neck
like a lock and key on the Capulet balcony

treading water

sitting beneath the showerhead
a steady stream scalds my spine
trying to cleanse the turmoil away

you say you were doing the same
just minutes ago

if we're both treading water
at least we'll be together when we drown

the author

she made worlds
within words

confused

like the sun shining
through a magnifying glass
scorching a white piece of paper
glassy-eyed kaleidoscope sight
looking with new luster
icy hair and stare compel me
stage presence but it's no act
tinted haze or fleeting flame
extinguished
anguished
languished
or unperished
sirens started something
I can't quite name

wasting water

lay my head against the clouds
let me cure this California drought

I don't drink anymore

it's been four months since I've had a drink
what do you call it when you abstain
not for any reason
but simply because you don't want to

why would I want to
when my head swirls on the pillow
and on the inside too
convinced that I'm speeding down Mulholland at midnight
no map, no headlights, no seatbelt, no brakes

serotonin drained like my tub with a broken plug
a sour cherry pit in my stomach
acid coating my throat teeth and gums
pain like a dull knife in my belly
even worse in my head

hollow time
tired mind

I don't drink anymore (reprise)

it's been nine months since I've had a drink
what do you call it when you abstain
not for any reason
but simply because you don't need to

why would I need to
when you make me feel the same
as any mule or merlot

flushed and rapturous
wasted on your taste
I'm a wallflower by choice
a live wire under your influence

never been addicted
to anything
until you

autumn east

I don't know what happens to us
when we die
whether there's a hell or heaven
but Vermont in October
is pretty damn close to the latter

you ruined dating for me

if we ever end
my standards will be
ripped to shreds

how I used to be

craters consume me
where explosive impacts left their mark
for a brief moment, we connect
aligned
but I move at a pace too fast for the world
if I don't stop spinning
I'll never have to know a solar eclipse

heavenly bodies

I see women on my screen
stretch marks on hips
cellulite on thighs
curves of the spine
that let me know they're alive

what a beautiful thing
to admire
when I see her
in the mirror

the other seasons

Shakespeare compared his love to a summer day
but you remind me of fall
when the leaves change color
so they're winsome and new
and the air is fresh and pure

or maybe winter
with your rosy cheeks
ruddy as if from the cold
it smells of cranberry and mint
and angels are in the snow

no, you're spring
welcomed in like an old friend
warmth settles in, long overdue
children wish on dandelions
and their petals swirl through the sky

the view

steering down side streets to avoid the traffic
ended up taking longer in the end
took three wrong turns and made one 360
then you remind me to look out the window
at the rolling hills by our side
and time is left in the dust

growing pains

I thought I'd cry less the older I got
no more falling from monkey bars
skinned knees from untied laces
or getting out in tag
but now I have overpriced rent
a boss who asks too much
politicians who love guns
and hate my favorite drag queens
writer's block, a reading slump
and the constant fear that I'm not enough

reeling

I teased
"I can't believe your world
doesn't revolve around me"
"oh but it does," you said "there are just
some other moons
and gravitational pulls, too"
it was all one big joke
but warmth flooded my face
the whole way home
I've never felt an ache so deep in my bones

female gaze

black rings around eyes
downturned chin
a mole on a cheek
I think of when I shouldn't

the female gaze is the simple answer
but what if it's more?

winter wonderland

I made my first snow angel
with you by my side
gingerbread crumbs on the counter
where we built a house together
homemade pasta and apple cider
you held my hand as we spun around
got snowed in
and missed our flight
but I didn't mind
it gave us more time
I'd never seen trees
so blanketed by white

dizzy

given me no reason
to doubt you're anything but what you say
still I find myself dizzy
from the circles my mind runs in,
the turns my pacing feet make
anxiety and romanticism
are like oil and water

therapy

I've known my therapist since I was twelve
she started as my Sunday school teacher
where we talked about
the philosophy of values

I guess I needed more practice

been seeing her for a while now
working on the things I don't like
I grew up too fast
I resent that fact

I'm a mass of contradictions
keep my distance
with anxious attachment
too stiff and too soft

there's no grading this time
so how do you measure
intangible matters?
am I allowed to be proud
when I'm not done growing
and I don't know if I ever will be?

honeycomb

the earth becomes air
I am a feather in the wind
I know safety when bare
a feeling yet to find
yellow lights I cease
there is no rush home
he is bliss and peace
sweet like honeycomb

the good

you are
a worn-in sweater and new knit blanket
a warm house with jazz in the kitchen
the sound of rain and lamps with an amber glow
soft white lights wrapped around pine
cinnamon sugar toast
crickets chirping on a starry night
birds singing on a Sunday morning
the smell of new books and my mom's cooking
a freshly made bed
candles
coffee
kiwi
and everything else
that I love

nobody likes you when you're twenty-three
and I don't like anyone either

you lied to me for the first time
and I went back in time
to the girl who was second-best
three times in a row

thirty minutes on the phone
ten of them in silence
then crying turns to laughter
and restoration calls in

this age is like an LA road
cursing, potholes, whiplash
at least you're sitting shotgun
how the hell did we get here?

coffee and anxiety don't mix but I drink it anyway

sitting in a cafe
sipping something hot
like a latte topped
with saccharine foam
I savor it
I'm safe

but my heart starts spinning
the blue open sign becomes blurry
and now I'm left to wonder
if I'm dying
or it's just the caffeine

a conversation in the dark

"I like you so much, I'm scared."
"scared?"
"that it's going to go away."
"well, then I'm scared too. we can be scared together."

2020

was I wasting time or just getting by
if I don't write to cure my feelings
am I even a real writer?
it's just that there were too many thoughts
for my pen to keep up with
and all I wanted was to mute them
I didn't feel like plotting any rising action
when I had enough conflict of my own

circles

you were a late summer baby
and your mom got to pick which grade
if she chose differently, you said to me
"we never would have met"
now the butterfly effect
keeps me up at night
wondering what if
I fed into my fear
and denied the invite
what if your sister
hadn't been in town
you stayed home on the couch
instead of showing her around
what if I had prolonged
the inevitable split
wasn't there all alone
you would've been pawned
what if I hadn't made that joke
the one that drew you in
a secret ingredient
that worked to provoke
or what if you never met my best friend
the winter before college
so you weren't there that night
or if I never met her
spring before freshman year
and sat together on that flight
or if I went to New York as I planned
or if you stayed in Colorado after all
or what if you weren't or
what if I wasn't or
what if

what if

what if

what if

what if

what if

what if

what if

what if

what if

what if

what if

what if

what if

what if

what if

what if

what if

what if

what if

what if

what if

what if

what if

what if

what if

what if

what if

what if

what if

what if

what if

what if

crying on my birthday

the first time I was younger, maybe ten or twelve
at the happiest place on earth
my sister ran off
she was always running back then
sat on a bench with fireworks raining down on my eyes
tear-stained iris in iris
muddled pops of magenta and azure
filled the warm California night air

the next a decade later
dinner is fine
the food is weak and the drinks strong
I have two for twenty-two
we go back to his place
I sit alone as he groans
scrubbing the kitchen counter
while I'm sick in the bathroom he just sits by the door
on my back I can feel his eyes
I shrink beside myself on the floor as they scrutinize

I'm sorry that my party interrupted your bad mood

ex-extrovert

protected my peace too much
and everyone slipped away

could use more voices
that aren't my own

Maplewood

turning left onto the avenue
everything is right
when I'm paces from you
the construction zone
and narrow road say hello
you come into view
then I melt in your embrace
and standing there on Maplewood
I'm where I belong

the wrong kind of manifesting

everyone keeps talking about manifestation
but I think I misread the instructions

over and over I say
he's going to forget me

then plead not to speak it
into existence

melodies

grace's voice rings in my ears until they bleed
her harmony makes me feel anything but
I stretch my hands out the sunroof
flying across West Hollywood
accelerating through red lights
til I collide with concrete

the apartment next door

when I first came over it was still just dust
a thin layer of dirt coating the ground
fall colors were everywhere
crimson leaves on branches
orange cones on the curb
I circled the block and you met me out back
you got me pink licorice
we watched Neve Campbell on screen
and that was the first time I felt your dark sheets

next came concrete
leasing soon signs in the grass
plaster and hardhats and "this could be your home"
you had become mine
the air was damp with summer
I got you a present
some brand-new blue shoes

today I see snapshots of people's lives inside
they've settled in, gotten comfortable
just like us now
there's a violet halo in one room
and vintage movie posters too

isn't it beautiful – the growth of it all?

cleanliness is next to godliness

if you ever want to feel
a little less sad
I find a hot shower
does wonders for the soul

a bad day's last straw

the end of the world
in the stub of a toe

haiku for my cat

a six-pound feline
satin fur, golden eyes wild
may have saved my life

punch drunk

apple of my eye
peach fuzz on your lips
I'm tongue-tied with a cherry stem
your taste is fine wine

the irony of the beach

watching waves crash on the sand
could soothe me for ten lifetimes
but the depths of the ocean
keep me up at night
questioning what's out there
that could pull me down

AMC

you and me at the movies
large popcorn to share
Sweet Tarts for you, Twizzlers for me
root beer for you, vanilla Coke for me

tonight we saw a re-release of Star Wars
I said "you can pick the snacks" as we got in line
you chose Twizzlers and vanilla Coke

we held hands while the trailers ran
and planned the next one we'd see
Thursday is my favorite tradition

I love you
you know

creative nonfiction

to tell you the truth
I've been embellishing my feelings

then again

no

I have my own
sun and moon

surrender

the difference between
defeat and acceptance
is mindset

existential crisis at the dentist

I had an existential crisis at the dentist's office
while reclining in a sage green chair
it's actually my favorite color
though I didn't like it much then
with the leaden taste of tools and blood in my mouth
is life just full of menial moments?
then on my drive home
the neon glow of sunset lit up the sky
on came a sweet song I'd never heard before
and suddenly I felt like I could make it to tomorrow

Milton Keynes UK
Ingram Content Group UK Ltd.
UKHW020923201123
432908UK00021B/3256